The Goddess Remembered

A Spiritual Journal

Illustrations by Melanie Lofland Gendron
Words by Melanie Lofland Gendron & Shawn Evans

The Crossing Press
Freedom, California 95019

ISBN 0-89594-448-0

A group of us, spurred on by Melanie Lofland Gendron and Shawn Evans, put this together with humility mixed with pleasure. We find the journal to be a prayer; may we, all of us, be endowed by the Goddess with happiness and hope.

Jane Somers, Elise Huffman,
Claudia L'Amoreaux, and Elaine Goldman Gill

Your daughters gather within thy sight to do thy will.

Wrap my heart in ceremonial robes that I may create abundance.

Sweet yonic rose, your honey nectar heals the lonely night.

Give me the grace to embrace the present, release myself from the past, and trust in the future.

Male and female are one, born of the great mother.

Meditating on a mountain, singing with my sister, it is easy to feel you inside of me. Come to me when it is most difficult to remember you and awaken me with your love.

Help me remember each motion is a sacrament.

Circle round to the east,
Circle round to the south,
Circle round to the west,
Circle round to the north.
Great spirit of our mother, come.
Great spirit of our mother, protect us.

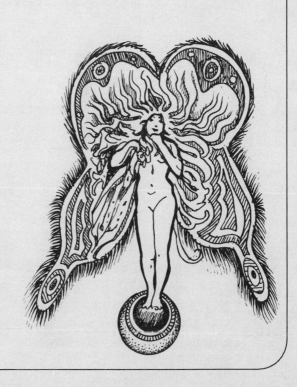

When you dance,
volcanoes pour forth molten lava,
hurricanes spiral over seas,
lightning bridges sky to earth.

Through pain I come to know.
Through joy I come to know.

Blessed be the power, knowledge, glory and beauty of thy manifestation on earth.

Your eyes hold me centered in myself.

As I follow your path, I slowly achieve balance.

Ancient sister, we dance again.

O Mother, make my body your temple.

Brilliance and shadow, birth and death, light and dark, you manifest opposites.

Every time I touch in love, I touch you.

A new baby's fresh milk smell causes the mother's heart to spill over.

You spin the thread of creation and weave the fabric of time.

We raise the chalice of holy breath.

Wordless, timeless, unlimited space,
no question asked or needed,
you hold me suspended in grace.

In your hands flows the universal life force.
My hands are your hands.
Guide them to heal, nurture, create.

Guide my dance, that I may circle in completion.

You are a weaver, spinning life with golden threads.

At rest, you feel a stir of desire and begin to dream of life.

You are the ebb and flow of tides, the waxing and waning of the moon. You are cyclic and eternal.

We are silent together.

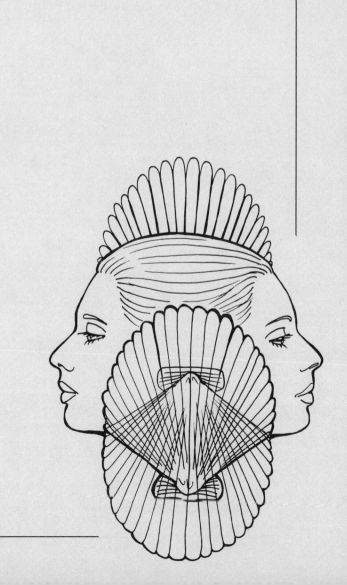

O holy one, keep me tight in thy embrace.

Your tears are healing rain.

In a spiral spinning, her daughters dance.
In a spinning spiral, her sisters chant.

First moon, first blood, quickening, quickening.
Quickening, quickening,
Each bud becomes a rose,
As we sing, as we sing.

Your fertile music sounds in thunder, rainstorms, wind
that blows pollen and seed.

Madonna of herbs and flowers, you fill the world
with holy musk.

O holy and sacred Mother, blessed is thy song Gaia.

Awaken your children from the darkness.
Help us to dance your dream of life.

Dearest mother, guide me home.

You birth galaxies and microbes in the same breath.
You love all equally without judgment.

You speak all languages.
Your skin is all shades.
Mother of the people —
Your blood flows in our veins.

Help me remember that I am one within the One,
and I am not alone.

As we spin an unbroken circle, may your song be on our lips.

Maya, you cast your net and I am caught in your illusion.

Your courage is my own.

Bless us with your grace. Relieve our suffering with the nectar of your compassion.

The immobile moves. All things change and rearrange to balance your universe.

I choose to gaze into my soul and know that I am goddess.

All nature sings your song.

Radiant one, thank you for the magic of life.

With one sound, you vibrate the universe.

Cloak thyself with the queen of light,
With starry sky and moondrenched night.

Your blood is my blood, your beauty my own.

Keeper of mysteries, you from whom all things flow, blessed life in thy presence.

All that live hear your call.

A few steps forward, a few steps back. Perhaps the purpose
is not so much heaven, but to learn to dance well.

Mother of shields, I stand firm in the strength of your love.

Hail the bright and fertile womb.

Teach me to ask for your gifts properly and to be grateful for what I receive.

Dancer of queenly grace, you evolve the universe.

Life Giver, to know you is to understand that death is but a veil.

Blessed be our great mother who has made me a woman.

You are the zodiac, clothed with the sun.

A compassionate sister, the sea.

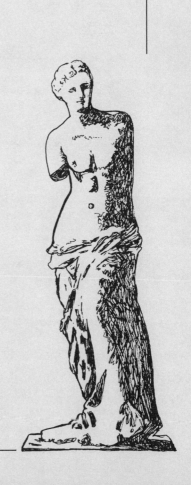

Your great womb is the source of all things.

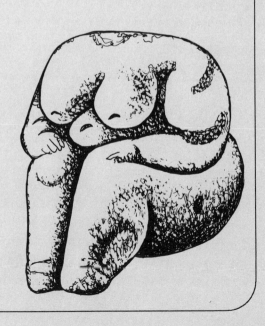

Goddess Divine,
Shed thy radiance in my heart and mind;
Fill my being with thy divine light
That it may shine in all my thoughts and actions,
And bring brightness to all.
Surround me with thy protecting love and abiding peace.